How to Draw BIRDS

Written and Illustrated by
Barbara Soloff-Levy

Watermill Press

Introduction

Welcome to the world of our fine-feathered friends! From the tiny hummingbird to the majestic eagle, the world of birds is a fascinating one. Long before mammals walked the earth, there were birds. The first bird lived 150 million years ago. It looked more like a lizard with feathers than the birds of today.

Today there are many kinds of birds. Some, such as the penguin and the ostrich, do not fly. Some, like the canary and the parrot, make wonderful pets. And others, like the hawk and the vulture, are fierce birds of prey. Would you like to draw these incredible creatures?

Start your drawing in pencil, so you can erase any unwanted lines. When your bird looks the way you want it to, go over your drawing with a felt-tip pen. Next, color it with crayons or colored markers.

Remember, the best part of your drawing is what you add to it with a little imagination—so make your birds any color you want. Don't be afraid to experiment. And, most of all, have fun!

Materials

(2) Number 2 Pencils
(2) Felt-Tip Pens
Eraser
Colored Markers or Crayons
Tracing Paper
Drawing Pad

Birds as Pets

Macaw Parrot

The macaw is the largest of all parrots. It has a long pointed tail and brightly colored feathers. Like most parrots, the macaw can talk!

Cockatoo

The cockatoo is also part of the parrot family. Although cockatoos rarely learn to talk, they often make loud screaming sounds!

Canary

The canary is the most popular of all bird pets. Their beautiful songs make them cheerful companions.

Parakeet

Parakeets are natural acrobats and can do many interesting tricks.

Lovebirds

Lovebirds are really small parrots. They are called *lovebirds* because they are so affectionate—they always stay close together.

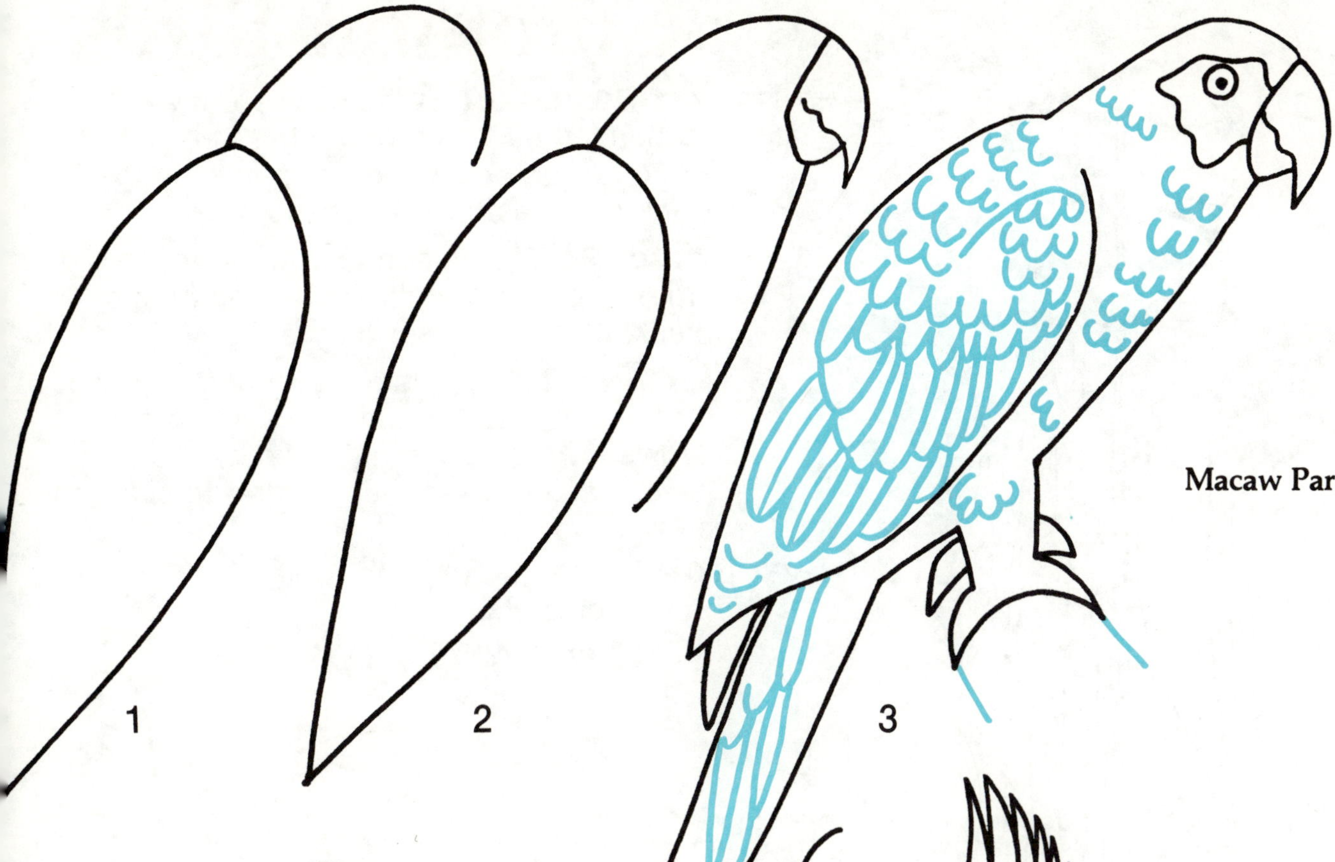

Macaw Parrot

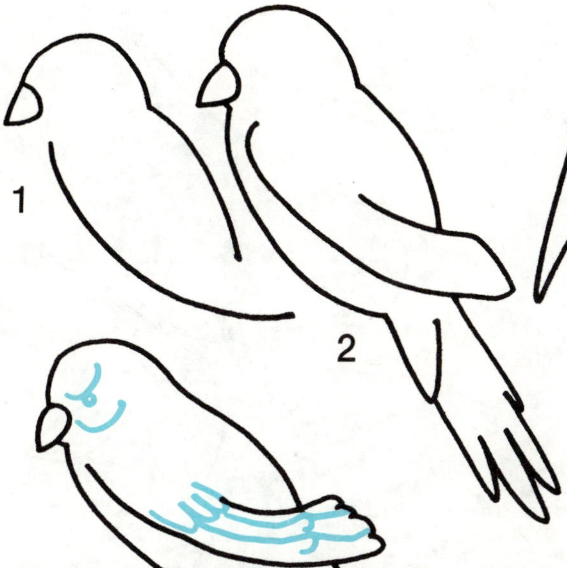

Canary

Cockatoo

Lovebirds

Common Birds

Woodpecker: Who's that funny redheaded bird up there in the tree? It's the woodpecker, noisily pecking holes in the tree trunk as it searches for insects.

Pigeon: The pigeon is often found in big cities. Most have dull-colored feathers of black, blue, brown, or gray.

Crow: The crow is a clever and fearless bird usually seen in meadows and orchards. Crows love to eat corn. That's why farmers have scarecrows in their fields—to scare the crows away!

Robin: The first spring robin is a welcome sign that winter is almost over!

Woodpecker

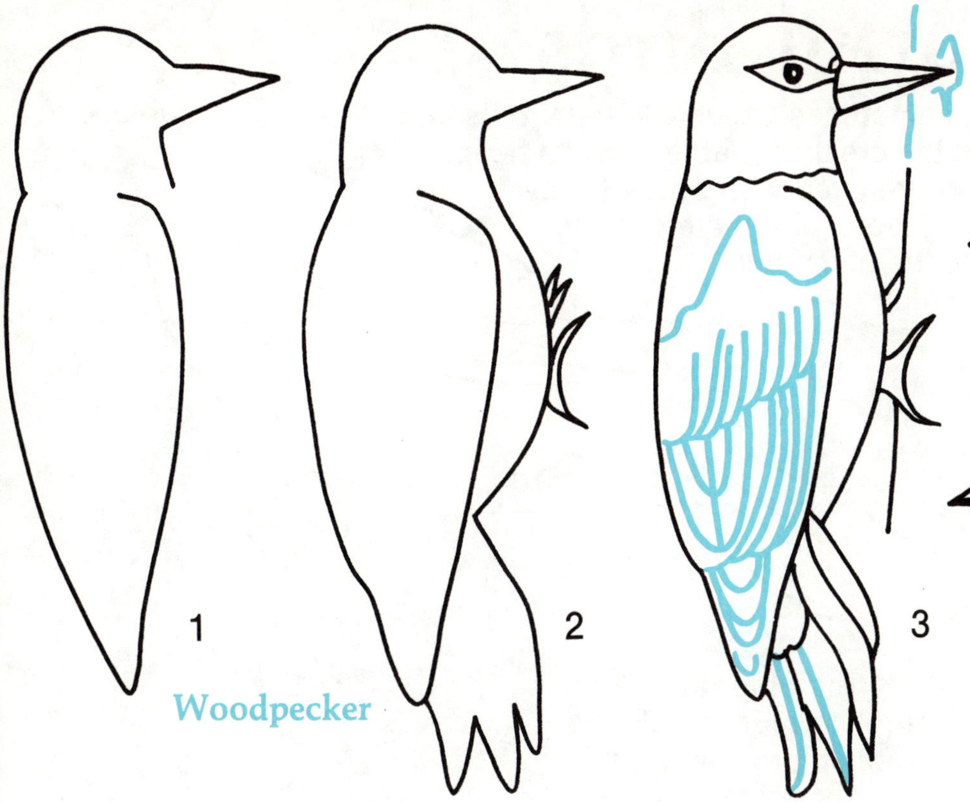

Robin

Crow

Pigeon

Colorful Birds

Cardinal: The cardinal, sometimes called the *redbird,* is known for its fiery red color and the crest of feathers on its head. The males are almost entirely red with tints of gray on their backs. The light-brown female has the crest and bill of the male, but little of its color.

Blue jay: The blue jay is known for its striking blue, black and white colors—and for its noise!

Hummingbirds: These tiny creatures get their name from the sound made by their wings which move 60 to 70 times a second.

Blue jay

Hummingbird

Cardinal

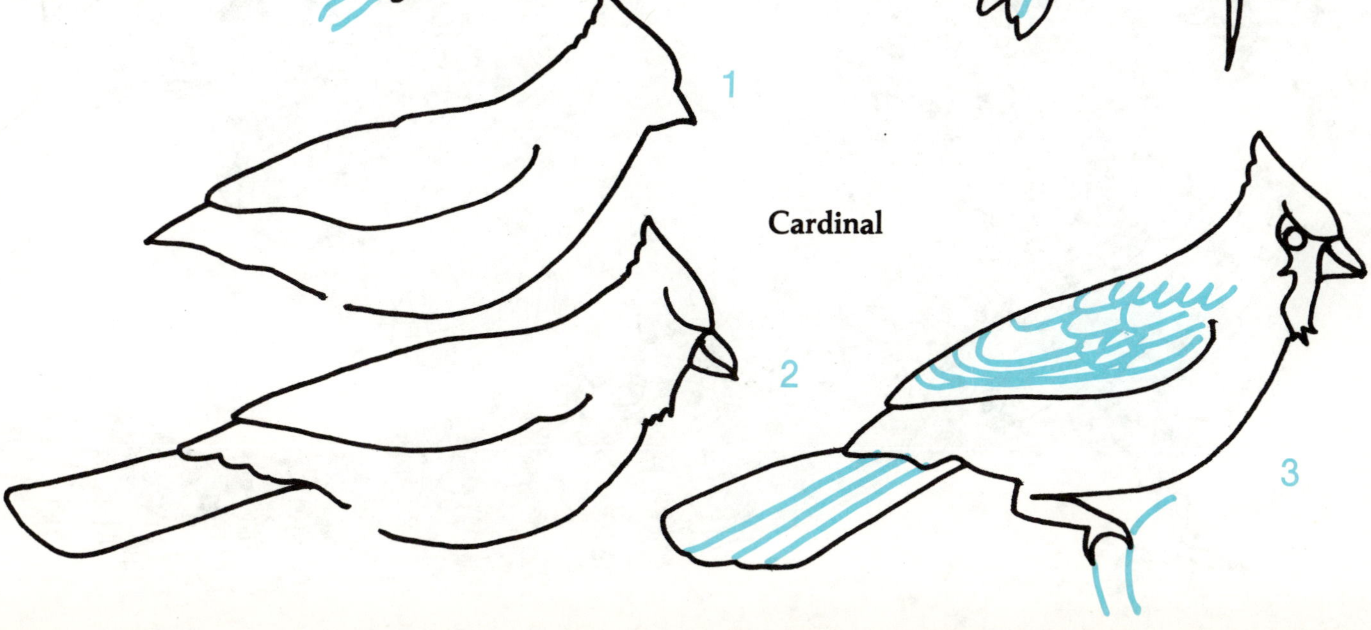

Colorful Birds

Peacock: The peacock is the showiest of all birds because of its great size and the beauty of its greenish-blue feathers. No one knows if the peacock is *really* proud of the way it looks. But the expression "proud as a peacock" is often used to describe someone who is proud.

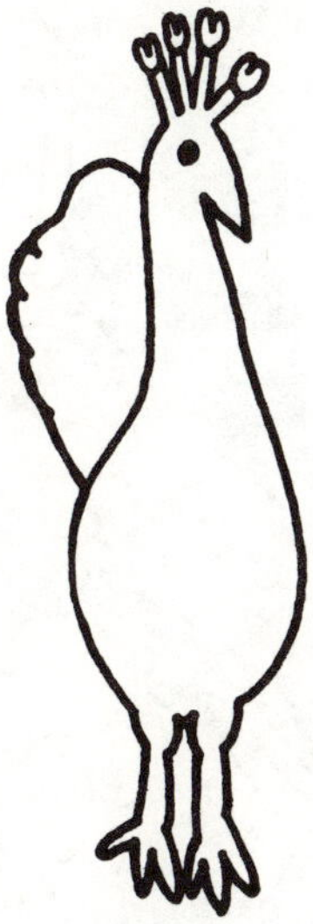

1

2

Feathers

1

2

3

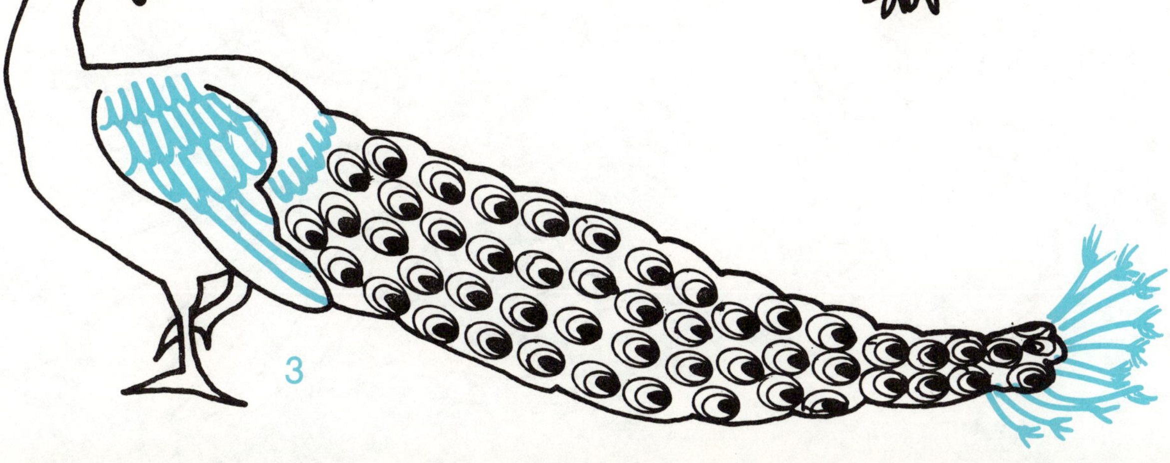

3

Game Birds

Rooster

The crowing rooster and the clucking hen are common barnyard sights. Many families keep small flocks of chickens to provide both meat and fresh eggs.

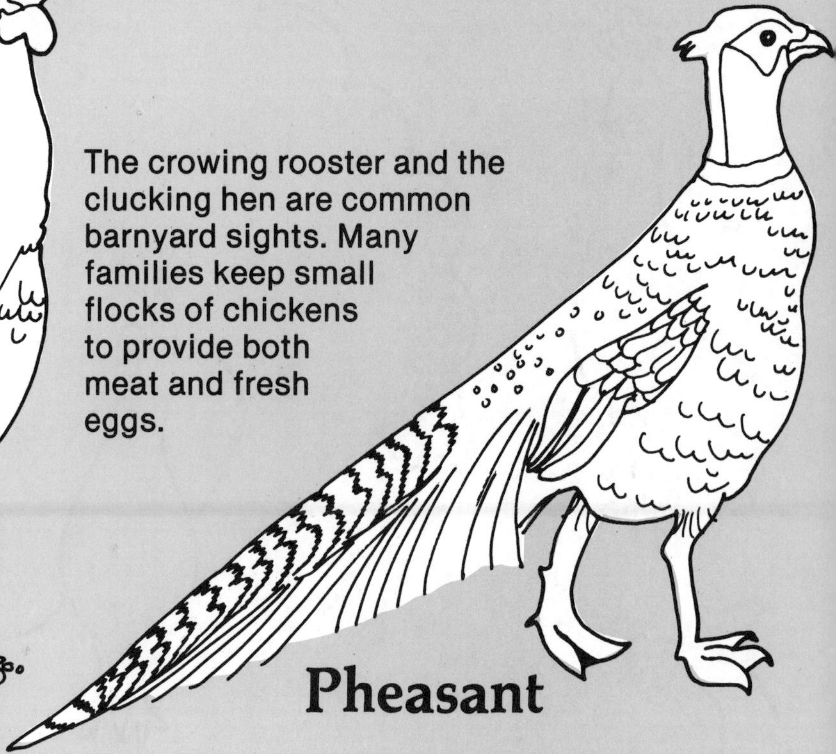

Hen

Pheasant

Both pheasants and turkeys are hunted in the wild for food and sport. This has caused certain kinds of pheasants to become scarce. Many wildlife preserves are trying to increase the number of pheasants by keeping them on protected land where they can't be hunted.

Turkey

Rooster
1
2
3
Turkey
1
2
3
Hen
1
2
Pheasant
1
2
3

Water Birds

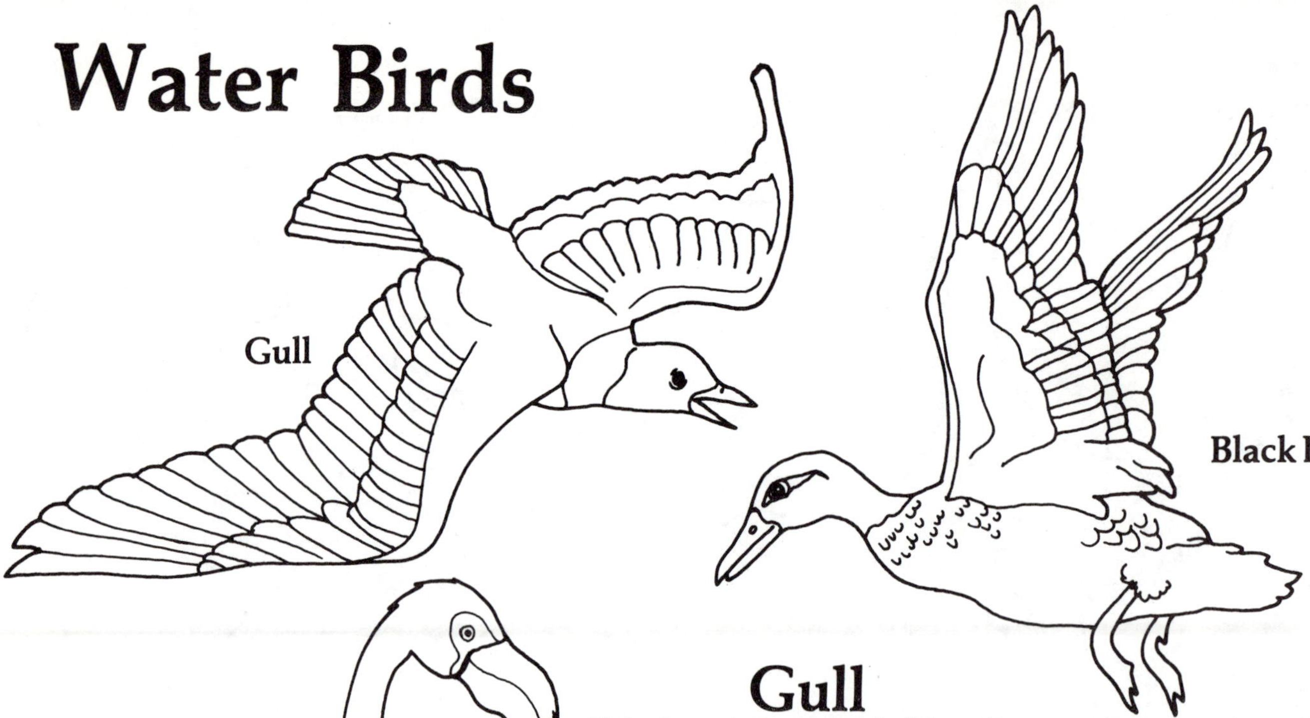

Gull

This long-winged bird is often seen swooping down over large bodies of water. Most gulls make their homes near the ocean, but some live near lakes and other inland waters. Gulls build their nests on rocky island ledges and in marshes.

Great Blue Heron

The Great Blue Heron is the largest wading bird in the United States. Herons build their nests in tree tops.

Flamingo

This graceful bird is known for its long legs and its curved bill and neck. Flamingos spend their entire lives near lakes, marshes, and seas. They build their nests by scraping together piles of mud.

Gull

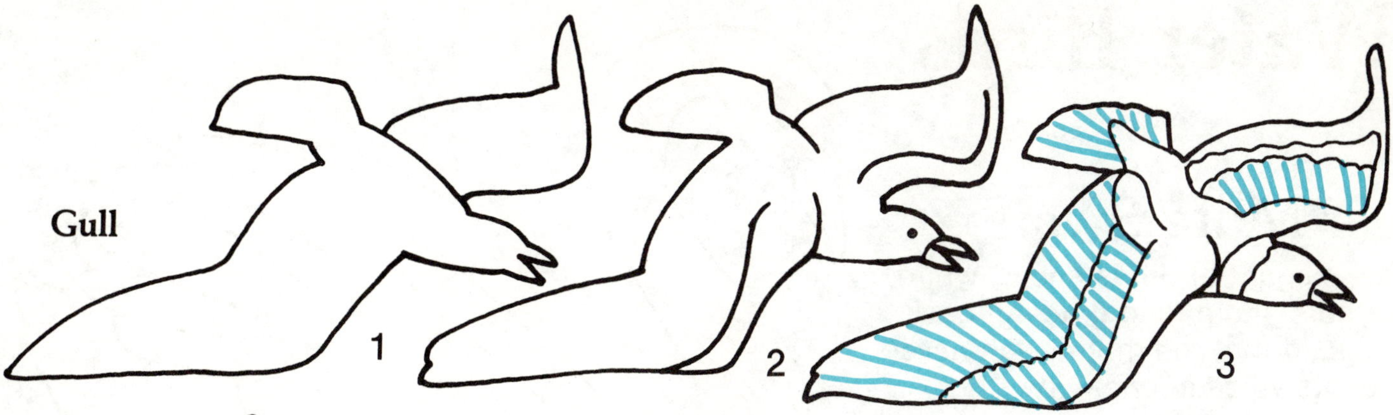

Black Duck

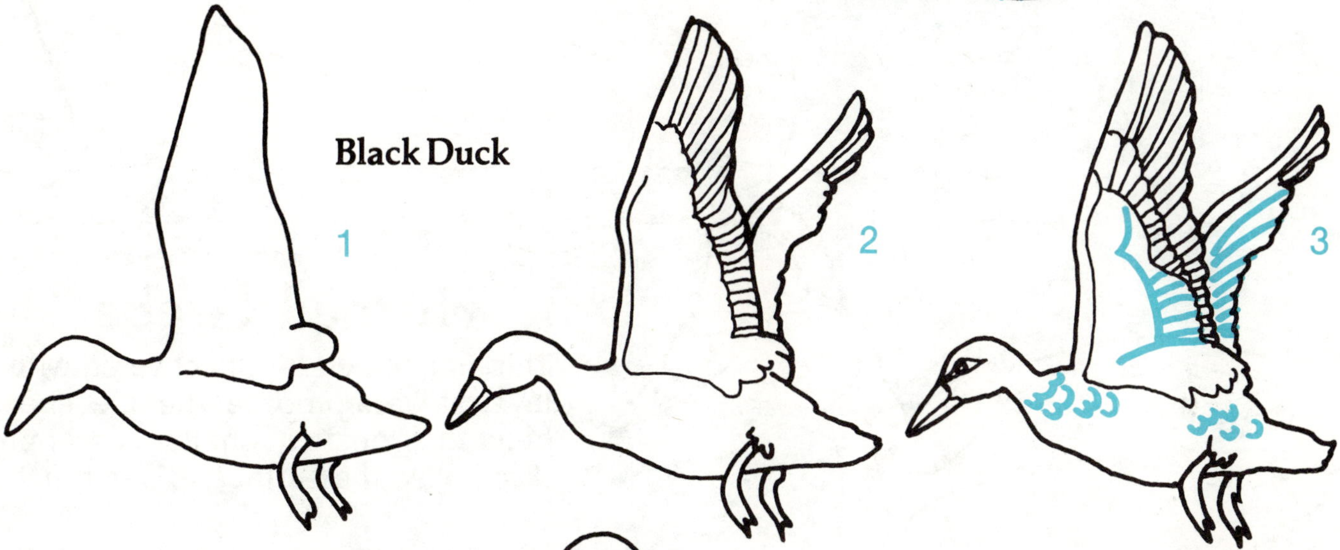

Flamingo

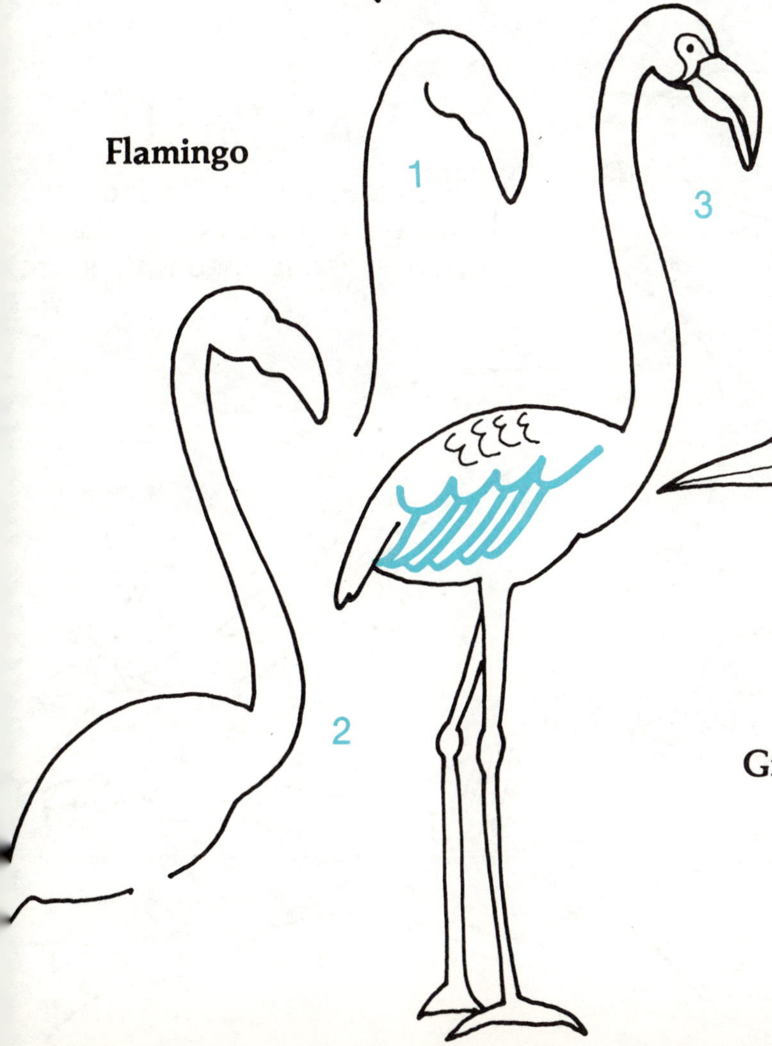

Great Blue Heron

Water Birds

Mute Swan

This elegant bird has snowy white feathers and a long graceful neck. It is said that the mute swan never uses its voice in captivity.

Horned Grebe

This flat-bodied bird is covered with a layer of waterproof feathers. Grebes build their nests in shallow water and dive below the surface to catch fish.

Wood Duck

The wood duck is an especially colorful bird. Like all ducks, the wood duck molts—or loses its feathers—in late summer. After molting, it flies south to its winter feeding ground.

Mallard

The mallard is a wild duck! Its nest is made of grass or weeds, and is lined with down.

Mute Swan

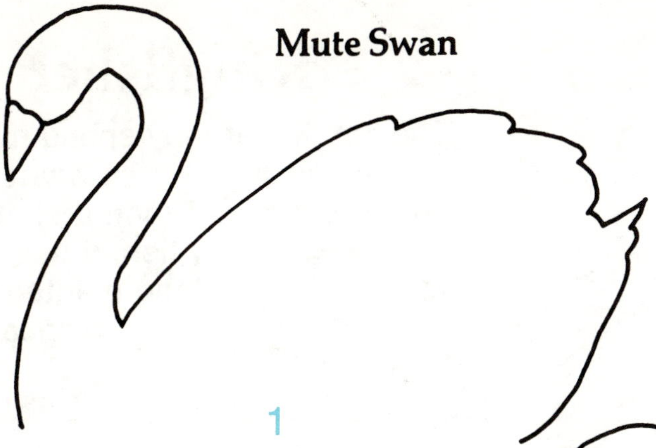

1

2

3

Horned Grebe

1

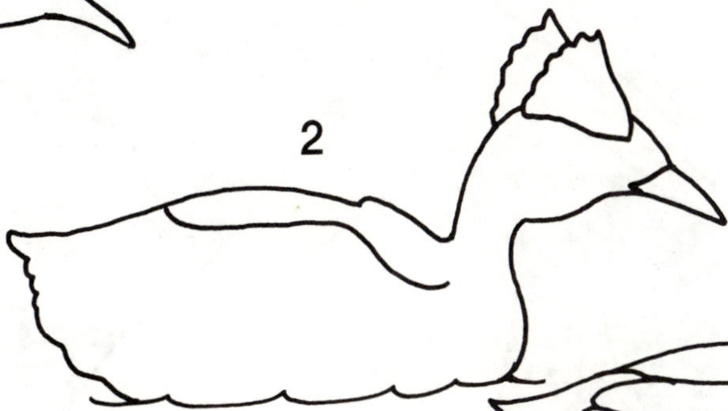

2

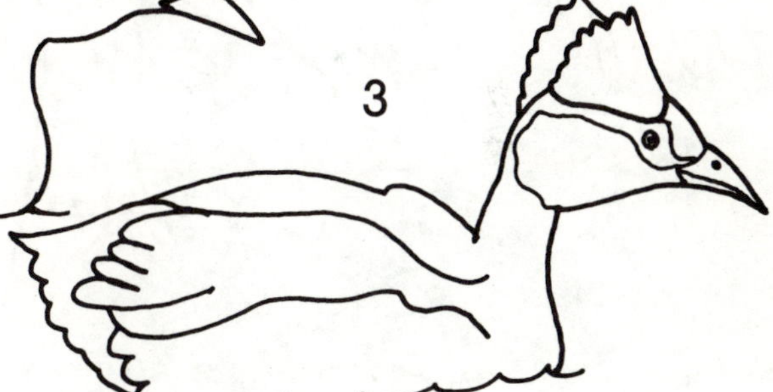

3

Wood Duck

1

2

Mallard

1

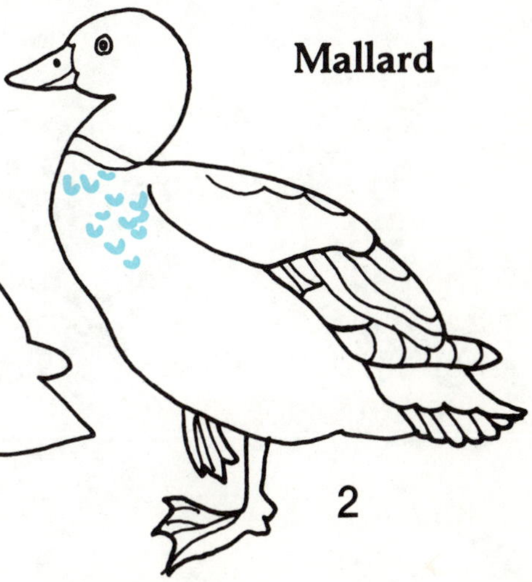

2

Water Birds

Kingfisher

The kingfisher may spend many hours sitting on tree branches over streams. When it spots a fish, it uses its long pointed bill to spear it.

Brown Pelican

The pelican is a strong graceful flier and a good swimmer, too. At the bottom of its bill is a fleshy pouch used to scoop up fish.

Kingfisher

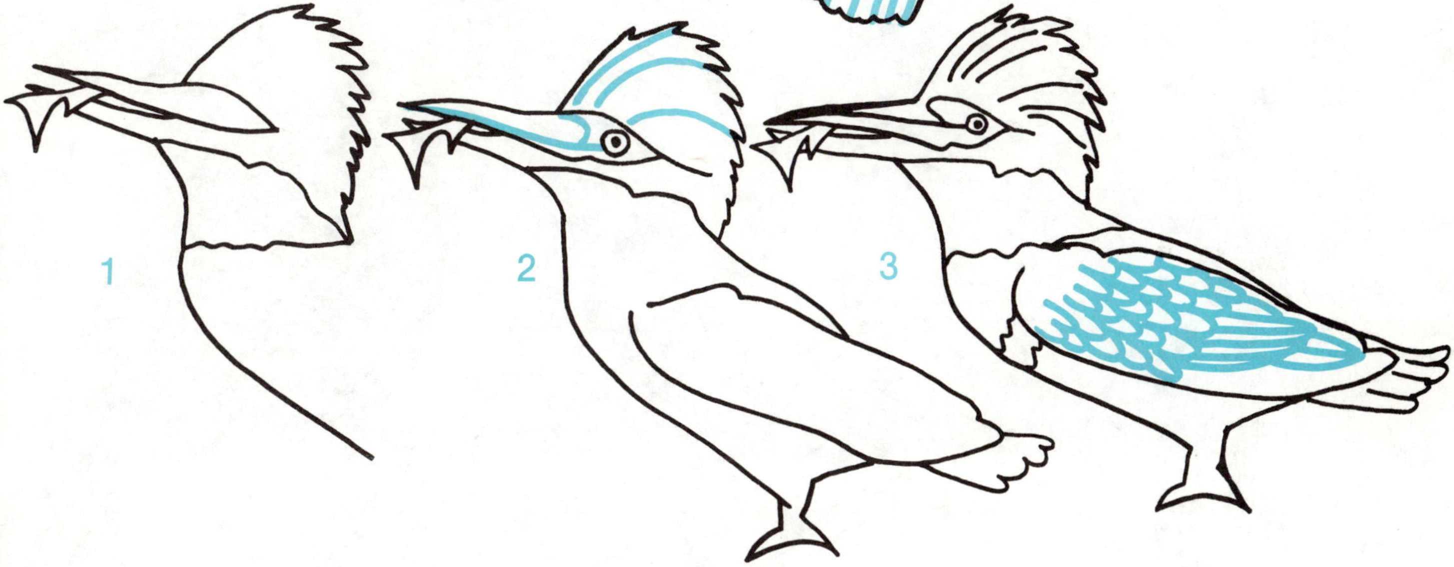

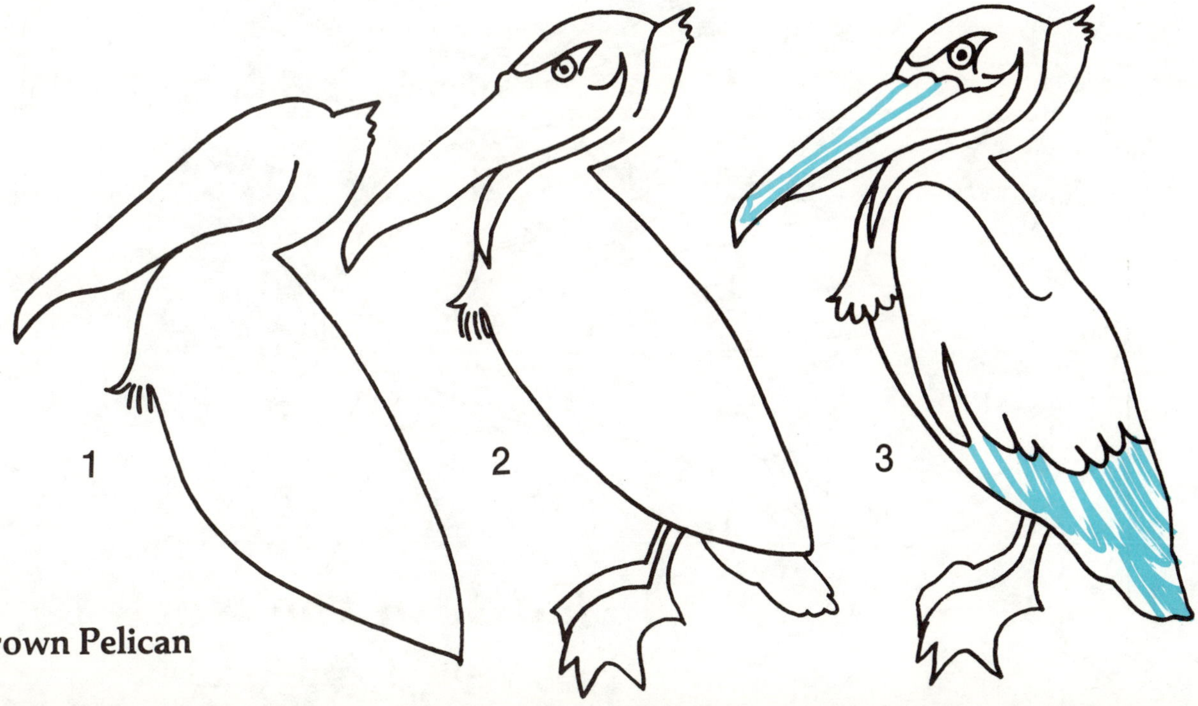

Brown Pelican

Birds from Other Lands

These birds have a beautiful array of colors to blend with their tropical surroundings.

Look at the picture of the rhinoceros hornbill. Can you see how it got its name?

Quetzal
(Central America)

Rhinoceros Hornbill
(Malaysia, Indonesia)

Cock of the Rock
(South America)

Quetzal

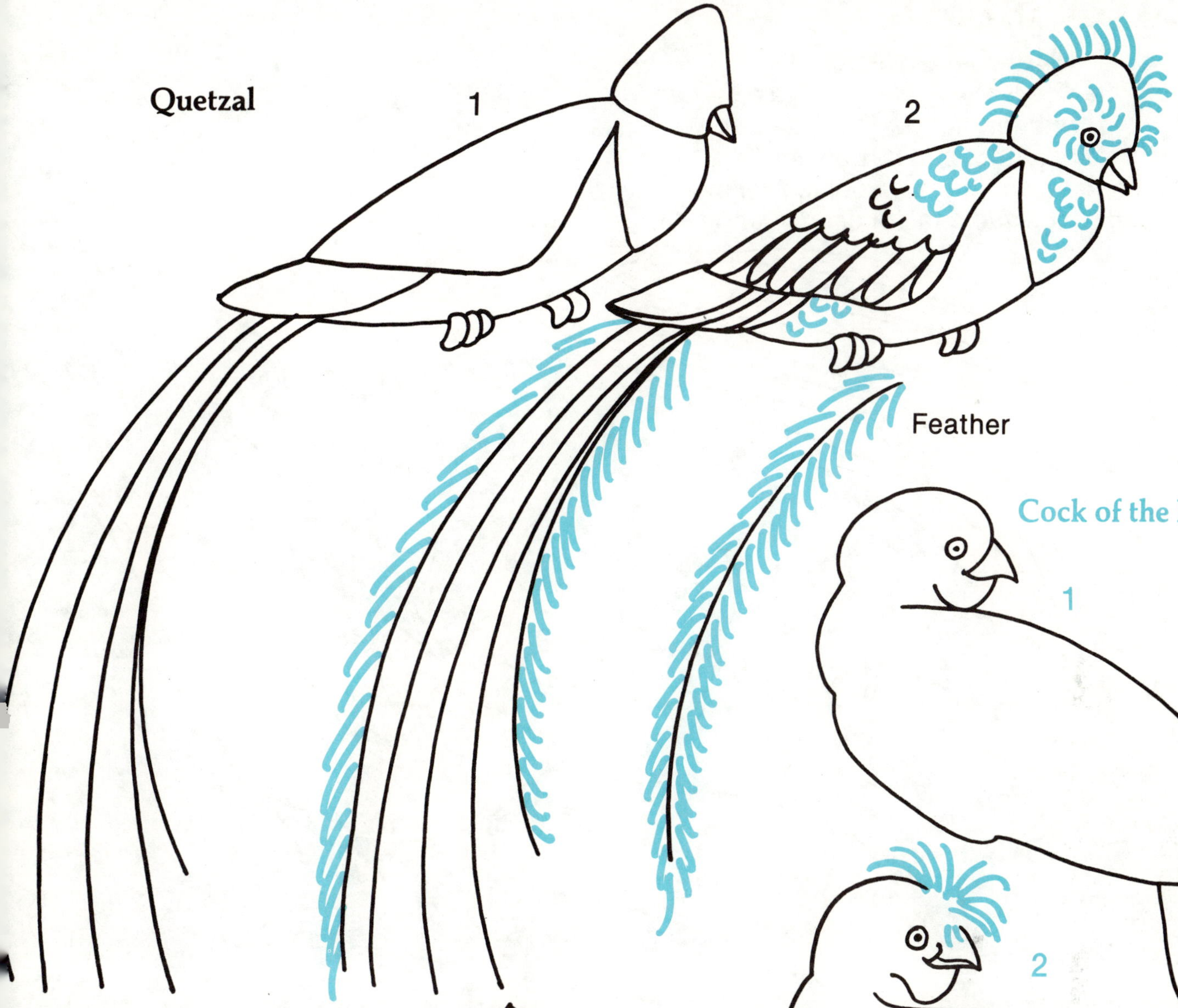

Cock of the Rock

Rhinoceros Hornbill

Great Bird of Paradise

(New Guinea)

Bird of Paradise is the name given to a certain kind of bird with feathers of many dazzling colors. This beautiful bird has an emerald green forehead and throat, a golden yellow head, and wings and a tail of deep maroon.

Skylark

(Europe)

Himalayan Monal

(Asia)

Toucan

(South America)

The toucan is an unusual-looking bird with an enormous, brightly colored bill. When it sleeps, a toucan turns its head around and places its bill down the center of its back!

Great Bird of Paradise

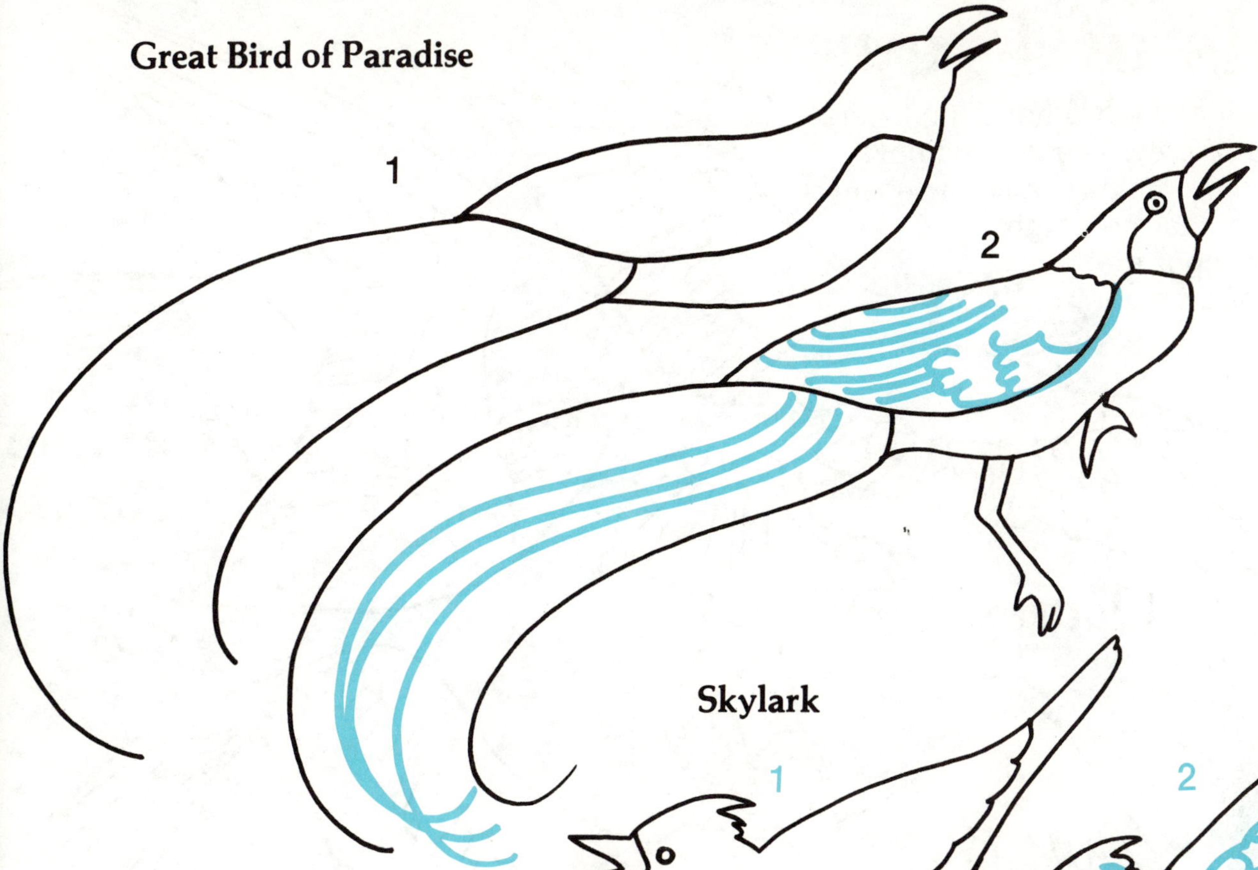

Skylark

Toucan

Himalayan Monal

Birds of Prey

Birds that kill and eat other animals are called *birds of prey.* These birds have powerful feet and claws, a keen sense of smell, and sharp eyesight to help them spot their prey from far away.

Osprey
1
2
Common Hawk
1
2
1
2
Turkey Vultures
Bald Eagle
1
2
1
2

Owls

Owls are hunters of the night. Unlike other birds, owls can see with both eyes at the same time. But, because they cannot move their eyes in their sockets, owls must turn their heads to see a moving object. The owls' eyes make them look as if they were wiser than other animals. Owls are known as symbols of wisdom.

Screech Owls

Barn Owls

Great Horned Owl

Birds that Don't Fly

Ostrich

Ostriches

The ostrich is the largest living bird. Like other flightless birds, the ostrich's ancestors *could* fly. But after thousands of years, the birds' wings became too small to support their bodies in the air.

On land, the ostrich is known for its speed. It can run as fast as 40 miles per hour!

Kiwi

Kiwi

This shy little bird lives in the forests of New Zealand. The kiwi, which is about the size of a chicken, is the only bird with nostrils at the tip of its bill. This helps the bird find food.

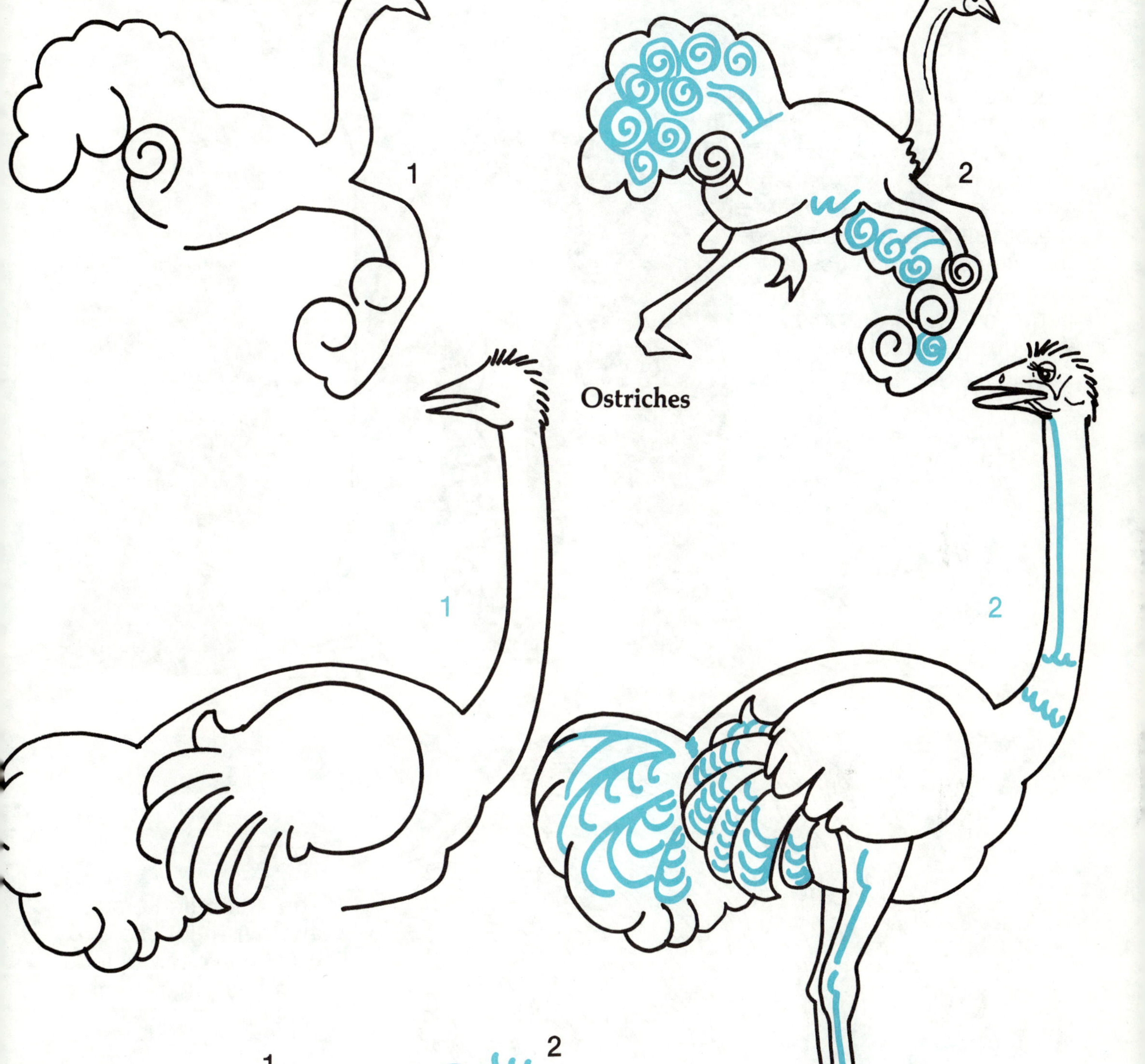

Ostriches

Kiwi

Birds that Don't Fly

Penguins

Most people think of penguins as birds in tuxedos! These funny little creatures, who have lost the ability to fly, are actually excellent swimmers. Millions of years ago, the penguins' wings developed into flippers, which act as paddles in the water. Most penguins live in the cold water of the Antarctic. But some can be found along the coasts of Australia, Africa, and South America.

Emu

The Australian emu is another flightless bird. It is known for its long legs and great running speed.

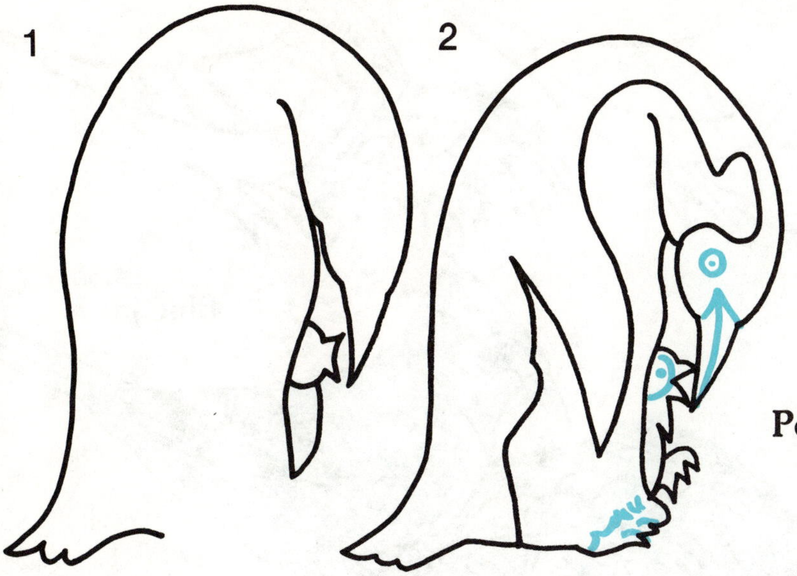

Penguins

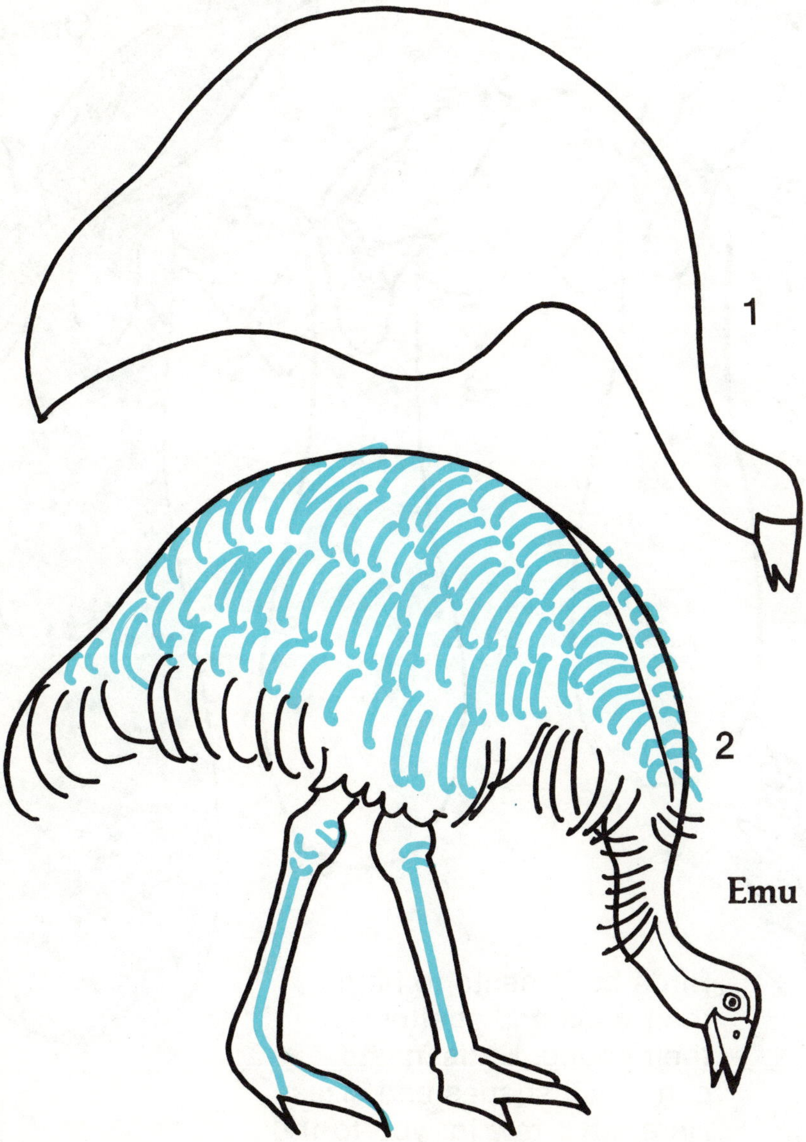

Emu

Birds Nesting

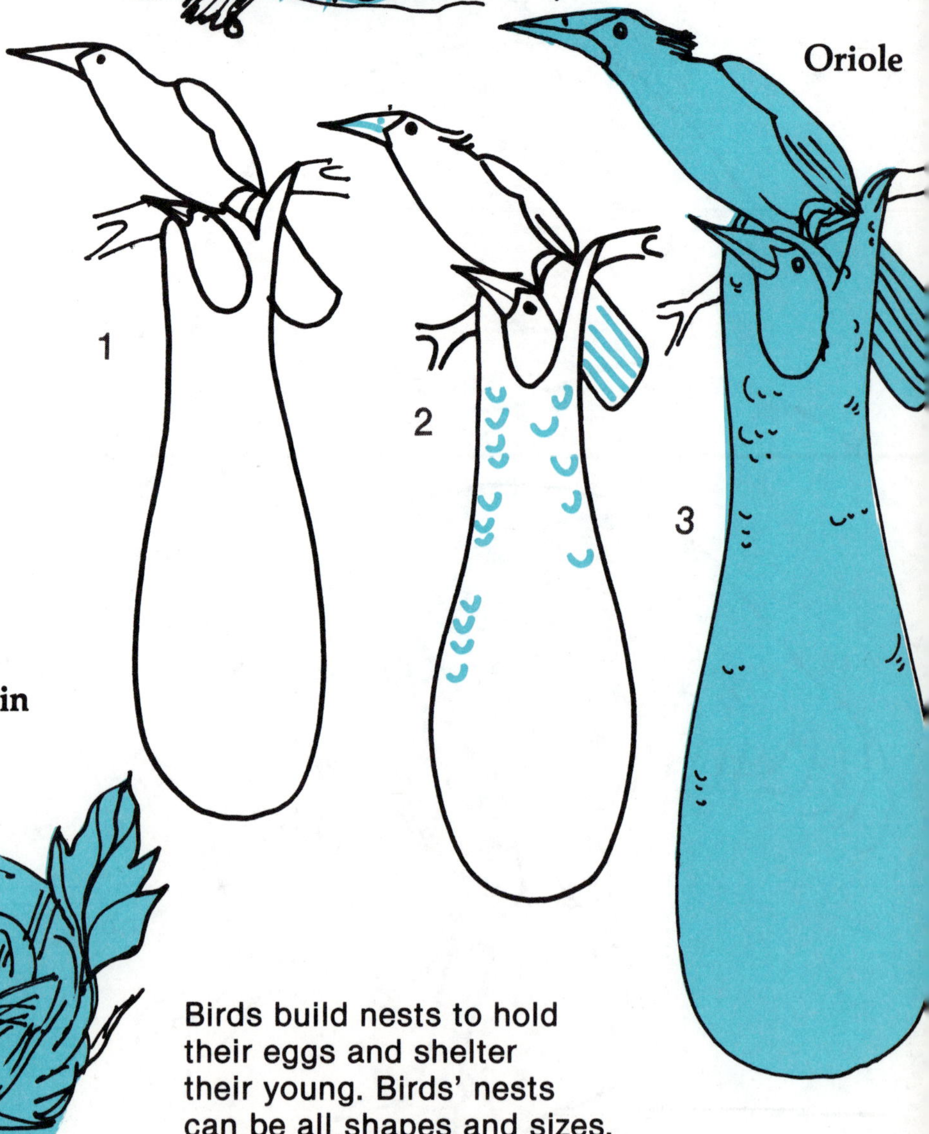

Birds build nests to hold their eggs and shelter their young. Birds' nests can be all shapes and sizes. Here are a few for you to try!